# Success Tips

## Things you didn't know about success

Coral Conquer

## Table of contents

## Chapter 1
## Is success subjective or objective?

### What Are You Measuring When It Comes to Success?

First, let's agree on a collective definition of success (for the sake of this article). A short Google search yields several subjective and objective definitions, many of which are at odds with one another. For instance, one of the most prominent definitions states, "The accomplishment of popularity or profit." You might be well-liked and make absolutely no money, or you can make some money and not be all that well-liked.

The first definition from the Oxford Dictionary that I found is an excellent one:
"The achievement of a goal or objective."

How can we determine whether we "accomplished our objective or purpose" then? Should we monitor progress depending on whether a profit is made? Do we want to utilize financial metrics as our initial metric?

How much is enough? is a question many of the financially "successful" individuals I know constantly ask themselves. Should we aim to earn millions? Only enough to purchase a home? Paying for our children's college tuition? Assemble a meal on the table?

Perhaps the best metric for success is how "happy" we feel after achieving our goal or purpose. Do we have a sense of accomplishment, fulfillment, and contentment upon reflection? Should the intensity of the sensation match the scope of the objective? For instance, at the helm of Facebook, Zuckerberg should "feel" as successful as someone with a brand-new firm making their first sale.

Because success is fundamentally a matter of opinion, quantifying it presents difficulties.

Even when the employees have been putting in late hours and weekends for seven years, many firms seem to "overnight succeed" and become wildly wealthy. Because we don't all share the same success criteria, benchmarking is challenging.

I primarily think that to be and feel "successful," one must define goals or purposes that are acceptable for their abilities, strive toward those goals despite hardship and sacrifice, and check off pre-determined measures for (personal) success at a pre-determined review time. Both objective and subjective measurements should be included, as I'll discuss below. But first, if you are reading this and thinking about your own "goal or purpose," I have two questions for you:

What drives you to start?

What motivates you, exactly?

It wouldn't be safe to start playing the comparison game and looking at what automobiles others are driving or what large property they live in if money isn't the primary motivator, would it?

If money is the primary motivator, realize that it is not a prerequisite for success. Financially "successful" people I know frequently don't feel successful or content with their circumstances.
I think that when this occurs, there is a fundamental misalignment in what is essential, which was a failure before the project, goal, or purpose even got off the ground. There was a misinterpretation of potential, no defined measures, and no apparent purpose.

Setting a goal or purpose that aligns with your potential should be your priority.

You must carry your potential. Think about this very carefully, and if you need a second opinion to see what you're capable of, ask your friends and family for assistance.

Objective Criteria for Success

Here, we're searching for closed-loop feedback metrics that can be monitored consistently and have a start and end date—trying to run a mile in less time? OK, start your stopwatch. Did you run more quickly this month than you did last? Trying to expand your company? Great, put money to use. Are you making more money this year than you did last year?

We may refer to them as Key Performance Indicators in business (KPIs). They consist of things like increased sales, client retention, number of new clients, market share, etc.

We may consider RHR, blood pressure, and several indicators for health, such as vitamin and mineral levels. To overcome the influence of our emotions, we want unbiased indicators of achievement.
They offer directions on how to get there. You'll experience highly high "highs" and extremely low "lows" as an entrepreneur. As an athlete, you'll experience both "on" days when you feel quick, agile, and powerful and "off" days. You will have days as a parent when you think you are doing well with your children and days when you feel you are failing them. In a way, objective metrics let us keep score and offer our goals to strive for.

Success Measures That Are Implied

We essentially seek contentment here. Do we believe we are progressing toward achieving our goal or purpose?

Subjective measures are challenging because we might unreasonably judge our performance as good or bad, which can cause the needle to swing in either direction—for instance, the innovator who tries hundreds of times before finally succeeding.

On the lightbulb, Thomas Edison is credited with saying, "I have not failed. I recently discovered 10,000 methods that won't work. People who fail in life frequently don't understand how close they are to succeeding when they give up.

You can never be sure. This is a terrifying concept since you might just as easily come up with 100,000 unsuccessful strategies.
To truly appreciate what we're doing, what we're doing, and how we're affecting the world, we must learn to break free from the cycle of accomplishment.

In this sense, "success" serves as a brief reminder to press on and keep up the good fight because it is worthwhile.

A client's recommendation, a student's grin, a hug from your child (simply to say I love you), and—most importantly—those butterflies in your stomach that make you smile as you walk down the street can all be seen as subjective markers of success.

Success, in my opinion, is only a pit stop along the more extensive journey of achieving your goal or purpose. It is the pursuit of defining an objective or purpose that aligns with your potential, pursuing that potential despite difficulty and sacrifice, and checking off KPIs at scheduled review intervals. Take responsibility for your potential, make goals that align with it, and start working. Soon after will come "success" in all of its aspects.

# Chapter 2
## Ways to measure success

Business success may be measured in various ways, including employee job satisfaction and the amount in a company's bank account. Finding out how you individually define your professional measure of success may be necessary, whether you're a cofounder of a business or have just begun working for a new company.

### What Exactly Is a Success Measure?

A benchmark by which a person or organization determines whether or not they have accomplished their objectives is known as a measure of success. Successful individuals utilize a range of standards to assess their individual and collective accomplishments since there is no actual definition of success.

Even if specific success indicators are more prevalent than others, they are at least partially arbitrary or relative. Even the highest-earning companies, for instance, may experience significant staff turnover, overburdened management, and a suffocating corporate culture. Due to its tremendous earning potential, some could consider such a firm successful. In contrast, others might argue that it falls short of their standards of success (due to its inability to foster a positive work environment).

### How Are Successes Measured?

The way you identify your main company goals will ultimately determine how you assess success. While you should align your goals with the general aims of the business, your measure of success should also make sense to you holistically.
Additionally, you may use a variety of criteria to determine success; for instance, achieving record profits and making sure your workers' going to work are not incompatible objectives.

Success may be gauged in at least two ways: qualitatively and statistically. You may assess success qualitatively by seeing broad company patterns that may be challenging to quantify quantitatively. Comparatively, quantifying success involves examining precise measurements, data points, and the like to assess how effectively your pre-determined objectives are being reached.
So, here are six ways you might describe success in your terms:

1. Establish your criteria.

Stop comparing yourself to other people's ideas of success. Decide what matters most to you in life; it might be fulfilling relationships, a fulfilling profession, or good health and fitness. Find a meaningful approach to gauge your success for each one after that.

2. Select the road leading to satisfaction.

If you aren't living the life, you intended to, all the money in the world, the perfect house in the neighborhood, and the most impressive job title won't mean a thing. Discover your life's purpose. Pay attention to your gut. And pursue inner fulfillment rather than pursuing external markers of life.

3. Pay attention to doing 1% more.

Setting objectives is vital, but once you know where you're going, it's time to concentrate on the individual steps of the route. You will get a little closer to achieving success each day if you commit to doing and giving a little bit more than you were willing to yesterday.

4. Establish ego-versus-intrinsic goals.

Choose the character traits you wish to develop while you work toward your objectives. Who do you want to develop into? What emotional muscles would you like to create? You may bring about genuine change and maintain your drive during trying times by developing success metrics that are fundamentally anchored rather than ego-based.

5. Spread the goodwill.

The most incredible sense of fulfillment might come from knowing that you have contributed to improving the world. When evaluating your accomplishment, consider if you have changed someone's life. Do my efforts contribute to the world around me being better?

6. Build your resilience.

No matter what your ultimate objective is or how you define success, there will be obstacles in your path. You'll make errors, and not everything will turn out as you expect. Whether you absorb the lessons from those blunders, keep going after setbacks, or give up on your ambition, determines whether you succeed or fail.

Passion, self-assurance, optimism, and the pursuit of a lifestyle that gives me what I've always desired—to be fully present for my children as they grow up, to know that I'm having a meaningful impact on others' lives, and to be firmly rooted in who I am and what I stand for—have all contributed to my experience of authentic happiness.

After all, isn't it part of what makes us human to want to believe that our lives matter? Don't we all want to know that we are making a difference in our lives and will leave the world a little bit better than we found it? Choose your criteria for success. Occupy them. And decide to live them now.

## Chapter 3

## How to be successful in life

What does success mean to you? How can one achieve success in life?

Success may be equated with many things by different people, including wealth, power, and having a positive impact on society. They're all accurate. Success may mean various things to different people. It would mean one thing to you but a different thing to someone else.

There are many books about success, yet each person's definition of success is different and personal. In what way might the same knowledge from each book be applied to all? Consequently, following the advice of a single individual is typically unproductive.

With this in mind, getting advice from many people, who may or may not have different definitions of success than you do, can be a fantastic place to start.

### 23 Strategies for Success

Here are 23 of the greatest quotes from some of the most accomplished people in history. The following success advice is essential if you wish to succeed:

1. Think broad.

Many people were affected by the great Renaissance artist Michelangelo Buonarroti.
Many years after his passing, his art still motivates and unites people. Consider the consequences if he had chosen not to become a professional artist. Would he have ever learned the secrets of success?

People commonly postpone their dreams in favor of something "realistic." they should abandon their ambition and choose something less complicated. Act with purpose instead.

## 2. Create a Schedule

"Your everyday routine contains the key to your future." Michael Murdock. Consider rising at the same time every day. Eat breakfast and make a strategy for the day. Find solace in knowing that you have some control over certain aspects of your life rather than feeling overwhelmed or harried. Finding your footing makes it simpler to tackle new problems and systemic issues.

## 3. Decide on your passion and pursue it

When attempting to figure out how to succeed at work, this quotation is a great one to keep in mind and give some thought to. Think about the potential success you may have in your current role. In the end, you'll probably discover that you must put a lot of effort and time into it.

Success in your career may imply that you will have to do more of the things you detest. What purpose does this serve? Why not pursue your interests? Once you've found your passion, you'll have more drive to keep moving forward. If you achieve this, your dreams will come true.

## 4. Discover Life Balance

People usually think that they must commit their entire lives to achieving their goals to succeed. People confident in their ability to succeed in work may put in long days and frequently late hours.
However, this comes at the sacrifice of enjoyment of life, health, and leisure. They can ultimately become exhausted and lose their professional effectiveness.

If their social life and friendships are the foundation of their success, their work may deteriorate, and they may lose their job, preventing them from going out with friends. As Knight points out, balance promotes success in several ways. Consider it a careful mix of rest, work, and enjoyment.

5. Be alone sometimes

"Not having to answer to anyone is the most pleasing thing about being alone. You carry out your wishes. — Justin Timberlake. Spend some time on yourself. Put the phone down, turn off the TV, and move away from the computer. Enjoy your "me time," and consider the things that brought you joy today. Or simply stop thinking. That is the charm of solitude. Your decision is yours.
On a bright day, spread a blanket outside, lie down, and enjoy the rejuvenating radiance. Keep in mind that every moment counts.

6. Don't worry about failing.

There is a story, and even if it's not sure whether it occurred, the lesson it conveys about success is still relevant: Thomas Edison invented the lightbulb after several unsuccessful efforts. He was interviewed and asked, "How do you feel after all of your fruitless attempts?" I discovered hundreds of methods not to create the lightbulb. Therefore I didn't fail, he said. Every "failure" taught him something. That lesson taught him what wouldn't and may work in its place.

Every failed attempt was an essential step on his path to success. It's simple to feel like giving up after a setback, but looking for a lesson in that failure could be a good idea. Pay attention and take notes when you experience setbacks.

7. Be steadfast in your determination to succeed

KFC founder Colonel Sanders said that there are many ways to learn from your failures.

Following a failure, giving up is simple. A sincere, burning desire to succeed and standing firm in your commitment to your goals are the only things that will keep you going. Success is difficult; it could seem unattainable without a relentless will to achieve it. When you have the motivation to figure out how to be more successful, it's merely a challenge to get over.

8 Never Allow Others to DefineYou

This quote resonates with me: "Be who you are and say what you feel because those who mind don't matter, and those who matter don't mind."- Bernard M. Baruch.
Why would we ever choose to exist in a society where everyone is similar to us? Could you imagine not having a say in what you wear, what you listen to, or what you like doing for fun? Each of us is special.

Yes, we all have our peculiarities, but at the end of the day, you can't let them define who you are. Never allow others to determine who you are or what you should do. They are free to decide how they live, not you. They are not worth your time, even if they try. If you want to learn how to be successful in every area of your life, surround yourself with people who accept you for who you are.

9. Be an active person.

Leonardo da Vinci spoke those words hundreds of years ago, yet they are still true today. Think about this Think about a person like William Shakespeare. We view the era in which he lived through his eyes when we consider it. When we think of Renaissance Italy, we immediately see Michelangelo and Leonardo da Vinci. Think about modern-day icons like Steve Jobs or Bill Gates. If they hadn't succeeded in what they did, modern life would be drastically different now.

You're most likely reading this on a device created by a company they founded or inspired. These folks were proactive; they saw chances to act differently and seized them. Instead, they helped to mold it. If you want to figure out how to succeed, don't be afraid to veer from the norm. If you can come up with a better way to do something, do it. If you fail, try again.

10. Plan everything.

Scheduling entails sticking to a schedule and completing the tasks that are intended to be completed. Successful people understand there is no time to put off what needs to be done immediately. They adhere to their timetables and are pragmatic about the meeting.

Procrastination is one of the most significant disruptions to a productive day, and successful individuals know this. Make a list of everything you want to do in a day rather than putting it off. You'll feel more accomplished and see how much time you'll need for everything else if you cross items off your list.

11. Foster a Positive Social Life

The most outstanding leaders and some of history's most significant figures were always kind to the people around them. They got favorable reviews. They wanted them to be successful. Effective leadership requires this. It is logical. You never know who could be able to help you out a lot or even just be a great and encouraging friend. Therefore, be good to others, and they will be kind to you. Help others, and they will help you.

12. Obtain Enough Rest

Successful individuals know that they need to get enough sleep to perform at their best. To be ready to start working the next day, the body must be recharged and reactivated. They don't stop themselves from getting the necessary slumber to re-energize themselves.

It's critical to understand the potential obstacles to sound sleep. A restful night's sleep might be hampered by using devices while lying in bed, consuming meals rich in sugar before bed, or remaining under a lot of stress all day. Before turning in for the evening, take care of them.

## 13. Do not be Afraid to Present New Concepts

Sadly, sometimes those with the most audacious ideas are passed over. Most of us are taught to think and behave like everyone else, beginning at a young age. But to act differently, you must think differently (as all great individuals did). When you have an original notion, embrace it rather than tossing it out because it is unique and different. One day, your strange new idea could hold the secret to your success.

## 14. Have faith in your abilities to succeed

If you want to learn how to be successful, you must be able to picture your success. A living example of such was Walt Disney. There may undoubtedly be others who doubt your capacity for success. You must resist falling into this category because your goals will be lost if you stop dreaming and believing in yourself. Dream away!

## 15. Be Daring

If you want to learn how to succeed at work, don't be scared to get in and attempt new things. Ask yourself, "What could go wrong?" For instance, you could not like shellfish. When your friend offers you sushi, you decline out of fear. Maybe this sushi has a lemon poppy seed coating over the white tuna and fresh strawberries. You're a fan of strawberries.

If you never had sushi, how would you know you detested it? What could go wrong? You expel it. Risks are part of life. The only way to find out is to try.

16. Consistently Keep a Positive Attitude

This was a declaration made by Thomas Jefferson, America's third president. As indicated in the phrase mentioned above, you must believe in your ability to succeed. The only way to cultivate a good mindset is in this way. Positive thoughts should take the place of negative ones. Challenges must be viewed as tasks to be completed rather than as impediments to your development.

If you remain upbeat and think this way, setbacks won't upset you as much, people's skepticism won't worry you, and even the most significant obstacles will seem minor. If you have the wrong kind of uncertainty, stopping will be much easier.

17. Be bold or leave home

Go above and beyond what is necessary and embrace your abilities and talents. Have a paper revised, evaluated, and submitted by Thursday if you have a form that needs to be turned in to your supervisor by Friday. Try a new dish and commit if you intend to bake for a picnic. Work hard and establish your merit if you want to get that huge promotion.

If you strive for achievement, you cannot fail. Even if you don't succeed or win, at least you try. You demonstrated grit, an admirable quality that cannot be imitated.

18. Don't Let Discouragement Get in the way

We all have some uncomfortable self-doubt, which is a negative feature of human nature. This can get worse if other people have the same doubts we have. Giving up could seem like the best course of action when faced with uncertainty. Ignore your doubts. Ignore your feelings of depression.

19 Set priorities

Successful people prioritize doing their work very well. The drawbacks of multitasking include diminished work performance. Because they know that multitasking frequently hinders productivity, successful individuals prioritize and cut out activities that will not advance their achievement.

20. Be Ready to Put in Hard Work

You may be acquainted with the 10,000-hour rule or the adage "success is 1% inspiration, 99 percent perspiration." Whatever angle you choose, they all agree that hard work is the secret to real success. You'll never succeed if you don't strive and keep working toward your life goal.

21. Uphold the Code of Conduct

We aspire to own and know everything. On the other hand, we adhere to the idea that you only have responsibility for yourself and no one else. Your life has many facets to it. Look for ways you can give back to your neighborhood. Participate in a charity, join a volunteer organization, or lend a hand to someone in need.

22. Trust Your Gut Feelings

Signs that In ancient Greece, a group of oracles lived in Delphi. Everyone who desired advice or to predict their future, from the lowest members of society to the monarchs, flocked to them. The temple's entryway was inscribed with the phrase "know oneself."

You already know how to do anything if you sincerely believe in it and want it. If not, you could have a natural sense of what will help and hurt you. It's comparable to how your body may detect danger even when circumstances seem secure. You must have faith in your judgment if you want to learn how to succeed.

23. Show gratitude

Learn to connect with people if you want to know how to succeed. Successful individuals raise their sense of value and self-esteem by valuing others around them. They are welcome to express gratitude and appreciation for any favors received. This boosts their self-esteem and stimulates the part of their brain that helps them appreciate and fully use their surroundings.

Under challenging circumstances, it might be difficult to feel appreciative. Work with a thankfulness diary to begin going. Every evening, list three or more positive things that occurred. This will assist your brain in turning away from all the negative aspects of the day and toward the positive ones.

## Chapter 4

## Signs that you are already successful

Every one of us has experienced a time when we felt like nothing was going our way, no matter what happened. It's simple to critique your abilities in the profession or how you handle issues at home, and this can make it simple to lose sight of your achievements in life.

It can be simple to think that you are a failure when you act constantly and lack clarity, even while all of the evidence in your life—both emotionally and professionally—points to the opposite conclusion.

You'll probably never find the opportunity to truly appreciate your success and accomplishments if you spend all of your time putting out flames. You might not even be aware that you are already successful. Here are a few indicators that it is the case:

### 1. Your income does not dominate you.

Many people believe that they depend on their next paycheck to make things work for them. You are most definitely a success if you can live daily without worrying that you won't have enough money to last until the end of the month! Even if you can't buy a Rolex, you're still successful if you aren't living weekly.

### 2. You do not desire recognition.

We typically outgrow the desire for praise from family, friends, and coworkers in our teenage years. You are more successful than you may even realize if you aren't waiting around for the conventional pat on the back at work or home. A significant indicator of mental security is the ability to carry out your responsibilities without seeking praise.

3. Less drama happens to you.

Do you notice a quieter atmosphere in your life as you reflect on just a year? At both home and work? If so, you can generally consider your life to be relatively successful because the absence of chaos implies order and harmony.

4. You are prepared.

Structure and having a long-term plan to achieve where you want to be are the foundations of success. You are already doing quite well in life if you truly have a plan to follow to accomplish your goals. People rarely make plans in advance!

5. You yearn for more.

If you tend to demand more from every circumstance, even if you feel you're not succeeding very well in life, you are already on the right track. Ambition and a thirst for knowledge are signs of someone who is driven to improve themselves.

6. You are a morning person.

You are aware of the proverb. The early bird catches the worm. You cannot begin each day in the afternoon if you want to succeed in life. You may attribute a successful lifestyle and personality when you wake up eager to take on the day and bounce out of bed.

7. You engage in social activity.

Success typically manifests itself in a variety of ways, not only in terms of position or salary. People don't usually stick with poisonous personalities, so if you can engage in a range of social situations and groups, that points to a healthy and harmonious life.

8. You promote respect for others.

Success typically stems from your own life experiences, including overcoming challenges and hardships. One of the most crucial components of success is already in your control if you comprehend the importance of treating others with respect.

9. You want to be of assistance.

Once more, the value of your achievement in this world transcends the price of your car. Success is not far away if you can give others a firm foundation to build and serve as a pillar of support for your coworkers.

10. You have ambition.

Anyone who lacks the drive and determination to overcome obstacles will find it difficult to succeed. You are successful if you don't mind having your hands dirty and your sleeves rolled up.

11. You are confident without being haughty.

How someone conducts oneself makes a significant distinction between someone successful and someone who thinks they are successful. You are already a successful person if you can inspire others who are struggling and exhibit true humility for others.

12. You have retaliated.

We've already discussed how failure might be the turning moment that leads to success. Before you can go to the top, you must first hit bottom. An iron-willed person with the intelligence to thrive in life is one who can fight back from failure to success—any success.

13. You work to get better.

Many people get caught up in the delusion that they "made it." You are positioning yourself for long-term success when you always strive to outperform your prior performance, no matter how spectacular it was.

14. You're disciplined

Only success and knowledge of how things have previously worked can bring discipline. Success over the long run requires learning to avoid errors and make the correct decisions.

15. You advise perseverance.

The most successful individuals exhibit patience on a vast scale. It might be difficult to ever have the influence you initially anticipated in any professional or interpersonal setting if you lack patience.

16. It's OK to refuse.

We have discussed the importance of being able to live without seeking praise; this is the same objective. The drive to please everyone can be avoided if you say "no." This is a trait of a successful person.

17. You're a good time manager.

Being able to use the time in any given day to be productively is a sign of success, and time management is an indication of long-term success. Able to manage a variety of jobs in a single day? You are successful already.

18. Your buddies are successful.

The most straightforward approach to motivating yourself is to observe success around you. It may be simpler to genuinely advance and develop yourself properly if you are surrounded by others who are succeeding.

19. You don't assign blame.

At this stage in your life, you get entirely what it means to take responsibility for your actions and stop blaming others for your problems and setbacks. Being proactive rather than passive and realizing your innate ability to change your life will lead to that. It also refers to your capacity to stop the environment from pushing you in a negative path.

20. You avoid wasting time.

The days of letting people force you to engage in time-consuming activities that you found dull or detrimental to your growth and self-esteem are long gone. You no longer require the approval of others since you have a stronger sense of direction.

21. You are confident.

You know that answering "yes" or "no" is insufficient. For people to see that you are an individual with your wants and opinions, you must clearly explain your reasoning. This does not imply being rigid, but you should never allow somebody to change their mind while being empathetic.

22. You maintain your optimism.

You've discovered that using negativity or skepticism to excuse probable losses and failures is useless. It not only makes you feel helpless and frightened, but it also has an impact on the outcome. You can bring out your genuine achiever by pursuing your goals with positivity and honesty.

23. You look for your well-being.

A significant first step is to quit engaging in detrimental behaviors that prevent you from working toward the better future you have dreamed of. You realize that giving up any bad habits—smoking, using drugs, eating excessive amounts of sugar and saturated fat, or not exercising—will make you stronger with more desire and willpower.

24. You don't look for a partner to help you with your problems.

It is simple to hide our shortcomings behind someone we love. But for both parties in a relationship to cease addressing the underlying problems that endanger one other's life is a little immature. It is not a good idea to refrain from assisting others in improving themselves just because it is simpler to do so or because "things are just great as they are."

25. You're an adult.

When negative working scenarios arise, you must deal with the person you have an issue with. Setting aside personal issues for career advancement is a sign of success.

Always remember that success isn't something that can be measured in terms of material possessions. You are already far more successful than any pat on the back would ever make you feel if you could look at your lifestyle and see that you act maturely, friendly, and productive.

Success comes from accepting your talents and abilities, not from what you are told by someone you may have never met before.

Conclusion

You may have noticed that many previous courses are comparable in that they all center on developing the right mentality. This clearly shows that your mental attitude is the key to success in your task.

Furthermore, you can succeed and make a difference no matter where you are.

www.ingramcontent.com/pod-product-compliance
Lightning Source LLC
LaVergne TN
LVHW020545160826
845677LV00015B/4215
*9798357881922*